50 Dairy-Free Ice Cream Recipes for Home

By: Kelly Johnson

Table of Contents

- Classic Vanilla Dairy-Free Ice Cream
- Chocolate Coconut Milk Ice Cream
- Strawberry Banana Nice Cream
- Mint Chocolate Chip Coconut Ice Cream
- Peanut Butter Swirl Dairy-Free Ice Cream
- Almond Milk Espresso Ice Cream
- Blueberry Lavender Dairy-Free Ice Cream
- Salted Caramel Cashew Ice Cream
- Mango Coconut Dairy-Free Ice Cream
- Raspberry Ripple Almond Milk Ice Cream
- Lemon Sorbet
- Pistachio Dairy-Free Ice Cream
- Chocolate Hazelnut Dairy-Free Ice Cream
- Pineapple Coconut Sorbet
- Cherry Almond Dairy-Free Ice Cream
- Matcha Green Tea Coconut Ice Cream
- Blackberry Coconut Milk Ice Cream
- Mocha Almond Fudge Dairy-Free Ice Cream
- Peach Sorbet
- Cookies and Cream Dairy-Free Ice Cream
- Raspberry Sorbet
- Chocolate Peanut Butter Dairy-Free Ice Cream
- Coconut Lime Dairy-Free Ice Cream
- Maple Walnut Dairy-Free Ice Cream
- Orange Creamsicle Dairy-Free Ice Cream
- Blueberry Banana Coconut Milk Ice Cream
- Vegan Rocky Road Ice Cream
- Pumpkin Spice Dairy-Free Ice Cream
- Chocolate Chip Cookie Dough Coconut Ice Cream
- Strawberry Rhubarb Dairy-Free Ice Cream
- Coconut Mango Dairy-Free Ice Cream
- Salted Caramel Chocolate Dairy-Free Ice Cream

- Kiwi Sorbet
- Cherry Chocolate Chip Dairy-Free Ice Cream
- Pineapple Basil Dairy-Free Ice Cream
- Raspberry Coconut Milk Ice Cream
- Vegan Butter Pecan Ice Cream
- Lemon Poppy Seed Dairy-Free Ice Cream
- Chocolate Covered Strawberry Dairy-Free Ice Cream
- Coconut Pineapple Sorbet
- Blueberry Cheesecake Dairy-Free Ice Cream
- Raspberry Lemonade Dairy-Free Ice Cream
- Coconut Rum Raisin Dairy-Free Ice Cream
- Chocolate Mint Dairy-Free Ice Cream
- Strawberry Kiwi Sorbet
- Key Lime Pie Dairy-Free Ice Cream
- Mango Pineapple Coconut Milk Ice Cream
- Vegan Snickers Ice Cream
- Lemon Basil Dairy-Free Ice Cream
- Hazelnut Chocolate Swirl Dairy-Free Ice Cream

Classic Vanilla Dairy-Free Ice Cream

Ingredients:

- 2 cans (13.5 oz each) full-fat coconut milk
- 1/2 cup granulated sugar
- 2 teaspoons vanilla extract
- Pinch of salt

Instructions:

1. Ensure that the cans of coconut milk are well chilled in the refrigerator overnight.
2. Once chilled, open the cans of coconut milk without shaking them. Scoop out the solid coconut cream that has risen to the top and transfer it to a mixing bowl. Reserve the coconut water for other uses or discard.
3. Add the granulated sugar, vanilla extract, and a pinch of salt to the coconut cream.
4. Use a hand mixer or stand mixer to beat the mixture on medium-high speed until it becomes smooth and creamy, and the sugar has dissolved completely. This should take about 2-3 minutes.
5. Taste the mixture and adjust the sweetness or vanilla flavor to your liking, if necessary.
6. Transfer the mixture to an ice cream maker and churn according to the manufacturer's instructions until it reaches a soft-serve consistency.
7. If you prefer a firmer texture, transfer the churned ice cream to a freezer-safe container, cover it with a lid or plastic wrap, and freeze for at least 4-6 hours, or until firm.
8. Before serving, let the ice cream sit at room temperature for a few minutes to soften slightly. Scoop into bowls or cones, and enjoy your classic vanilla dairy-free ice cream!

This recipe yields a creamy and delicious vanilla ice cream that's perfect for anyone looking for a dairy-free alternative. Feel free to customize it by adding mix-ins like dairy-free chocolate chips, chopped nuts, or fruit swirls.

Chocolate Coconut Milk Ice Cream

Ingredients:

- 2 cans (13.5 oz each) full-fat coconut milk
- 1/2 cup cocoa powder (unsweetened)
- 1/2 cup maple syrup or agave nectar
- 1 teaspoon vanilla extract
- Pinch of salt
- Optional: dairy-free chocolate chips or shredded coconut for topping

Instructions:

1. Place the cans of coconut milk in the refrigerator overnight to chill.
2. Once chilled, open the cans of coconut milk without shaking them. Scoop out the solid coconut cream that has risen to the top and transfer it to a mixing bowl. Reserve the coconut water for other uses or discard.
3. Add the cocoa powder, maple syrup or agave nectar, vanilla extract, and a pinch of salt to the coconut cream.
4. Use a hand mixer or stand mixer to beat the mixture on medium-high speed until it becomes smooth and creamy, and all the ingredients are well combined. This should take about 2-3 minutes.
5. Taste the mixture and adjust the sweetness or chocolate flavor to your liking, if necessary.
6. Transfer the mixture to an ice cream maker and churn according to the manufacturer's instructions until it reaches a soft-serve consistency.
7. If you prefer a firmer texture, transfer the churned ice cream to a freezer-safe container, cover it with a lid or plastic wrap, and freeze for at least 4-6 hours, or until firm.
8. Before serving, let the ice cream sit at room temperature for a few minutes to soften slightly. Scoop into bowls or cones, and top with dairy-free chocolate chips or shredded coconut if desired.

This recipe creates a rich and creamy chocolate ice cream with the tropical flavor of coconut milk. It's a delicious dairy-free treat that's perfect for chocolate lovers!

Strawberry Banana Nice Cream

Ingredients:

- 2 ripe bananas, peeled, sliced, and frozen
- 1 cup frozen strawberries
- 1-2 tablespoons maple syrup or honey (optional, depending on sweetness preference)
- 1 teaspoon vanilla extract (optional)
- Optional toppings: sliced fresh strawberries, banana slices, granola, chopped nuts, coconut flakes, or chocolate chips

Instructions:

1. Place the frozen banana slices and frozen strawberries in a food processor or high-powered blender.
2. Add the maple syrup or honey (if using) and vanilla extract (if using) to the blender.
3. Blend the ingredients on high speed, scraping down the sides of the blender as needed, until the mixture becomes smooth and creamy. This may take a few minutes and you may need to pause and stir the mixture occasionally to help it blend evenly.
4. Taste the nice cream and adjust the sweetness or flavorings to your liking, adding more maple syrup, honey, or vanilla extract if desired.
5. Once the nice cream reaches a smooth consistency, transfer it to a freezer-safe container.
6. If you prefer a firmer texture, you can freeze the nice cream for an additional 30 minutes to 1 hour before serving.
7. Before serving, let the nice cream sit at room temperature for a few minutes to soften slightly. Then scoop it into bowls or cones and top with your favorite toppings, such as sliced fresh strawberries, banana slices, granola, chopped nuts, coconut flakes, or chocolate chips.
8. Enjoy your delicious and healthy Strawberry Banana Nice Cream as a refreshing dairy-free dessert or snack!

This recipe is quick and easy to make, and it's a great way to enjoy the natural sweetness of fruit in a creamy frozen treat. Plus, it's customizable with your favorite toppings for added flavor and texture.

Mint Chocolate Chip Coconut Ice Cream

Ingredients:

- 2 cans (13.5 oz each) full-fat coconut milk, chilled overnight in the refrigerator
- 1/2 cup fresh mint leaves, chopped
- 1/2 cup maple syrup or agave nectar
- 1 teaspoon vanilla extract
- 1/2 teaspoon peppermint extract
- 1/2 cup dairy-free chocolate chips

Instructions:

1. Before you begin, make sure to place the cans of coconut milk in the refrigerator overnight to chill.
2. Once chilled, open the cans of coconut milk without shaking them. Scoop out the solid coconut cream that has risen to the top and transfer it to a mixing bowl. Reserve the coconut water for other uses or discard.
3. In a small saucepan, heat the chopped fresh mint leaves and maple syrup or agave nectar over low heat. Let it simmer gently for about 5 minutes to infuse the mint flavor into the sweetener. Remove from heat and let it cool slightly.
4. Strain the mint-infused sweetener through a fine-mesh sieve, pressing on the mint leaves to extract as much flavor as possible. Discard the mint leaves.
5. Add the cooled mint-infused sweetener, vanilla extract, and peppermint extract to the coconut cream. Use a hand mixer or stand mixer to beat the mixture on medium-high speed until it becomes smooth and creamy, about 2-3 minutes.
6. Taste the mixture and adjust the sweetness or mint flavor to your liking, if necessary.
7. Fold in the dairy-free chocolate chips until evenly distributed throughout the mixture.
8. Transfer the mixture to an ice cream maker and churn according to the manufacturer's instructions until it reaches a soft-serve consistency.

9. If you prefer a firmer texture, transfer the churned ice cream to a freezer-safe container, cover it with a lid or plastic wrap, and freeze for at least 4-6 hours, or until firm.
10. Before serving, let the ice cream sit at room temperature for a few minutes to soften slightly. Then scoop it into bowls or cones, and enjoy your Mint Chocolate Chip Coconut Ice Cream!

This recipe creates a refreshing and creamy dairy-free ice cream with a perfect balance of mint flavor and chocolate chips. It's a delicious treat for mint chocolate lovers!

Peanut Butter Swirl Dairy-Free Ice Cream

Ingredients:

- 2 cans (13.5 oz each) full-fat coconut milk, chilled overnight in the refrigerator
- 1/2 cup creamy peanut butter (unsweetened)
- 1/2 cup maple syrup or agave nectar
- 1 teaspoon vanilla extract
- Pinch of salt

Instructions:

1. Before you begin, make sure to place the cans of coconut milk in the refrigerator overnight to chill.
2. Once chilled, open the cans of coconut milk without shaking them. Scoop out the solid coconut cream that has risen to the top and transfer it to a mixing bowl. Reserve the coconut water for other uses or discard.
3. In a separate microwave-safe bowl, heat the peanut butter in the microwave for about 30-60 seconds, or until it becomes smooth and pourable. Let it cool slightly.
4. Add the maple syrup or agave nectar, vanilla extract, and a pinch of salt to the coconut cream. Use a hand mixer or stand mixer to beat the mixture on medium-high speed until it becomes smooth and creamy, about 2-3 minutes.
5. Taste the mixture and adjust the sweetness to your liking, if necessary.
6. Drizzle the melted peanut butter over the coconut cream mixture in the mixing bowl.
7. Use a knife or skewer to gently swirl the peanut butter into the coconut cream mixture, creating a marbled effect.
8. Transfer the mixture to an ice cream maker and churn according to the manufacturer's instructions until it reaches a soft-serve consistency.
9. If you prefer a firmer texture, transfer the churned ice cream to a freezer-safe container, cover it with a lid or plastic wrap, and freeze for at least 4-6 hours, or until firm.

10. Before serving, let the ice cream sit at room temperature for a few minutes to soften slightly. Then scoop it into bowls or cones, and enjoy your Peanut Butter Swirl Dairy-Free Ice Cream!

This recipe creates a creamy and delicious dairy-free ice cream with a swirl of rich peanut butter throughout. It's a satisfying treat for peanut butter lovers!

Almond Milk Espresso Ice Cream

Ingredients:

- 2 cups unsweetened almond milk
- 1/2 cup granulated sugar
- 2 tablespoons instant espresso powder or instant coffee granules
- 1 teaspoon vanilla extract
- 1/4 teaspoon almond extract (optional)
- Pinch of salt
- 1 tablespoon cornstarch
- 1 tablespoon cold water

Instructions:

1. In a saucepan, combine the almond milk, granulated sugar, instant espresso powder or coffee granules, vanilla extract, almond extract (if using), and a pinch of salt. Heat the mixture over medium heat, stirring constantly, until it starts to simmer and the sugar and espresso powder have dissolved completely.
2. In a small bowl, mix the cornstarch with the cold water until smooth to create a slurry.
3. Slowly pour the cornstarch slurry into the simmering almond milk mixture, whisking continuously to prevent lumps from forming.
4. Continue to cook the mixture over medium heat, stirring constantly, until it thickens slightly and coats the back of a spoon. This should take about 5-7 minutes.
5. Remove the saucepan from the heat and let the mixture cool to room temperature.
6. Once cooled, transfer the mixture to a bowl, cover it with plastic wrap, and refrigerate for at least 4 hours or overnight to chill thoroughly.
7. Once the mixture is chilled, pour it into an ice cream maker and churn according to the manufacturer's instructions until it reaches a soft-serve consistency.

8. If you prefer a firmer texture, transfer the churned ice cream to a freezer-safe container, cover it with a lid or plastic wrap, and freeze for at least 4-6 hours, or until firm.
9. Before serving, let the ice cream sit at room temperature for a few minutes to soften slightly. Then scoop it into bowls or cones, and enjoy your Almond Milk Espresso Ice Cream!

This recipe creates a creamy and flavorful dairy-free ice cream with the rich taste of espresso. It's perfect for coffee lovers looking for a refreshing treat!

Blueberry Lavender Dairy-Free Ice Cream

Ingredients:

- 2 cans (13.5 oz each) full-fat coconut milk, chilled overnight in the refrigerator
- 2 cups fresh or frozen blueberries
- 1/2 cup maple syrup or agave nectar
- 1 tablespoon culinary lavender buds (dried or fresh)
- 1 teaspoon vanilla extract
- Pinch of salt

Instructions:

1. Before you begin, make sure to place the cans of coconut milk in the refrigerator overnight to chill.
2. Once chilled, open the cans of coconut milk without shaking them. Scoop out the solid coconut cream that has risen to the top and transfer it to a mixing bowl. Reserve the coconut water for other uses or discard.
3. In a small saucepan, combine the blueberries, maple syrup or agave nectar, and culinary lavender buds. Bring the mixture to a simmer over medium heat, stirring occasionally.
4. Let the mixture simmer gently for about 5-7 minutes, or until the blueberries have softened and released their juices, and the mixture has thickened slightly.
5. Remove the saucepan from the heat and let the mixture cool to room temperature.
6. Once cooled, strain the blueberry mixture through a fine-mesh sieve, pressing on the solids to extract as much liquid as possible. Discard the solids.
7. Add the strained blueberry syrup, vanilla extract, and a pinch of salt to the coconut cream in the mixing bowl. Use a hand mixer or stand mixer to beat the mixture on medium-high speed until it becomes smooth and creamy, about 2-3 minutes.
8. Taste the mixture and adjust the sweetness or lavender flavor to your liking, if necessary.
9. Transfer the mixture to an ice cream maker and churn according to the manufacturer's instructions until it reaches a soft-serve consistency.

10. If you prefer a firmer texture, transfer the churned ice cream to a freezer-safe container, cover it with a lid or plastic wrap, and freeze for at least 4-6 hours, or until firm.
11. Before serving, let the ice cream sit at room temperature for a few minutes to soften slightly. Then scoop it into bowls or cones, and enjoy your Blueberry Lavender Dairy-Free Ice Cream!

This recipe creates a creamy and fragrant dairy-free ice cream with the natural sweetness of blueberries and a hint of floral lavender. It's a delightful treat for any time of year!

Salted Caramel Cashew Ice Cream

Ingredients:

- 2 cans (13.5 oz each) full-fat coconut milk, chilled overnight in the refrigerator
- 1 cup raw cashews, soaked in water for 4-6 hours or overnight
- 1 cup coconut sugar or brown sugar
- 1/4 cup water
- 1 teaspoon vanilla extract
- 1/2 teaspoon sea salt, plus extra for sprinkling
- Optional: chopped toasted cashews for garnish

Instructions:

1. Before you begin, make sure to place the cans of coconut milk in the refrigerator overnight to chill.
2. Drain and rinse the soaked cashews.
3. In a blender, combine the soaked cashews, coconut milk (just the solid cream part), vanilla extract, and 1/4 teaspoon of sea salt. Blend until smooth and creamy.
4. In a small saucepan, combine the coconut sugar or brown sugar and water over medium heat. Stir until the sugar has dissolved.
5. Bring the sugar mixture to a gentle boil and let it cook without stirring for about 5-7 minutes, or until it thickens and turns a deep amber color.
6. Remove the saucepan from the heat and carefully pour in the cashew-coconut milk mixture. Stir until well combined.
7. Let the mixture cool to room temperature, then transfer it to an airtight container. Cover and refrigerate for at least 4 hours or overnight to chill thoroughly.
8. Once chilled, pour the mixture into an ice cream maker and churn according to the manufacturer's instructions until it reaches a soft-serve consistency.
9. If you prefer a firmer texture, transfer the churned ice cream to a freezer-safe container, cover it with a lid or plastic wrap, and freeze for at least 4-6 hours, or until firm.

10. Before serving, let the ice cream sit at room temperature for a few minutes to soften slightly. Then scoop it into bowls or cones, sprinkle with additional sea salt and chopped toasted cashews if desired, and enjoy your Salted Caramel Cashew Ice Cream!

This recipe creates a rich and creamy dairy-free ice cream with the indulgent flavor of salted caramel and the nutty crunch of cashews. It's a decadent treat that's perfect for satisfying your sweet cravings!

Mango Coconut Dairy-Free Ice Cream

Ingredients:

- 2 ripe mangoes, peeled, pitted, and diced
- 2 cans (13.5 oz each) full-fat coconut milk, chilled overnight in the refrigerator
- 1/4 cup maple syrup or agave nectar
- 1 teaspoon vanilla extract
- Pinch of salt
- Optional: toasted shredded coconut for garnish

Instructions:

1. Before you begin, make sure to place the cans of coconut milk in the refrigerator overnight to chill.
2. In a blender or food processor, puree the diced mangoes until smooth. Set aside.
3. Once chilled, open the cans of coconut milk without shaking them. Scoop out the solid coconut cream that has risen to the top and transfer it to a mixing bowl. Reserve the coconut water for other uses or discard.
4. Add the pureed mangoes, maple syrup or agave nectar, vanilla extract, and a pinch of salt to the coconut cream. Use a hand mixer or stand mixer to beat the mixture on medium-high speed until it becomes smooth and creamy, about 2-3 minutes.
5. Taste the mixture and adjust the sweetness to your liking, if necessary.
6. Transfer the mixture to an ice cream maker and churn according to the manufacturer's instructions until it reaches a soft-serve consistency.
7. If you prefer a firmer texture, transfer the churned ice cream to a freezer-safe container, cover it with a lid or plastic wrap, and freeze for at least 4-6 hours, or until firm.
8. Before serving, let the ice cream sit at room temperature for a few minutes to soften slightly. Then scoop it into bowls or cones, sprinkle with toasted shredded coconut if desired, and enjoy your Mango Coconut Dairy-Free Ice Cream!

This recipe creates a creamy and tropical dairy-free ice cream with the sweet and vibrant flavor of mangoes combined with the richness of coconut milk. It's a refreshing treat that's perfect for enjoying on a hot day!

Raspberry Ripple Almond Milk Ice Cream

Ingredients:

For the ice cream base:

- 2 cans (13.5 oz each) full-fat coconut milk, chilled overnight in the refrigerator
- 2 cups unsweetened almond milk
- 1/2 cup maple syrup or agave nectar
- 1 teaspoon vanilla extract
- Pinch of salt

For the raspberry ripple:

- 2 cups fresh or frozen raspberries
- 1/4 cup maple syrup or agave nectar
- 1 tablespoon lemon juice
- 1 tablespoon water
- 1 teaspoon vanilla extract

Instructions:

1. Before you begin, make sure to place the cans of coconut milk in the refrigerator overnight to chill.
2. In a blender or food processor, blend the almond milk, maple syrup or agave nectar, vanilla extract, and a pinch of salt until well combined.
3. Once chilled, open the cans of coconut milk without shaking them. Scoop out the solid coconut cream that has risen to the top and transfer it to a mixing bowl. Reserve the coconut water for other uses or discard.
4. Add the almond milk mixture to the coconut cream. Use a hand mixer or stand mixer to beat the mixture on medium-high speed until it becomes smooth and creamy, about 2-3 minutes.

5. Taste the mixture and adjust the sweetness or vanilla flavor to your liking, if necessary.
6. Transfer the mixture to an ice cream maker and churn according to the manufacturer's instructions until it reaches a soft-serve consistency.
7. While the ice cream is churning, prepare the raspberry ripple. In a small saucepan, combine the raspberries, maple syrup or agave nectar, lemon juice, and water. Cook over medium heat, stirring occasionally, until the raspberries break down and the mixture thickens slightly, about 5-7 minutes. Remove from heat and stir in the vanilla extract. Let the mixture cool to room temperature.
8. Once the ice cream reaches a soft-serve consistency, transfer half of it to a freezer-safe container. Spoon half of the raspberry ripple mixture over the ice cream. Repeat with the remaining ice cream and raspberry ripple, creating swirls with a spoon or knife.
9. Cover the container with a lid or plastic wrap and freeze for at least 4-6 hours, or until firm.
10. Before serving, let the ice cream sit at room temperature for a few minutes to soften slightly. Then scoop it into bowls or cones, and enjoy your Raspberry Ripple Almond Milk Ice Cream!

This recipe creates a creamy and fruity dairy-free ice cream with the tartness of raspberries and the subtle sweetness of almond milk. It's a delightful treat for raspberry lovers!

Lemon Sorbet

Ingredients:

- 1 cup water
- 1 cup granulated sugar
- 1 cup freshly squeezed lemon juice (about 4-6 lemons)
- Zest of 1 lemon (optional)

Instructions:

1. In a small saucepan, combine the water and granulated sugar. Heat over medium heat, stirring occasionally, until the sugar is completely dissolved. This will create a simple syrup.
2. Once the sugar is dissolved, remove the saucepan from the heat and let the simple syrup cool to room temperature.
3. While the simple syrup is cooling, juice the lemons to obtain 1 cup of freshly squeezed lemon juice. You can also zest one of the lemons if you want to intensify the lemon flavor.
4. Once the simple syrup is cooled, stir in the freshly squeezed lemon juice and lemon zest (if using).
5. Pour the lemon mixture into a shallow dish or baking pan and place it in the freezer.
6. After about an hour, check the mixture. It should start to freeze around the edges. Use a fork to scrape the frozen edges and mix them into the liquid center.
7. Continue to check and stir the mixture every 30 minutes to an hour until it is completely frozen and has a smooth, sorbet-like texture. This process usually takes about 3-4 hours.
8. Once the sorbet is frozen to your desired consistency, transfer it to an airtight container and store it in the freezer until ready to serve.
9. Before serving, let the sorbet sit at room temperature for a few minutes to soften slightly. Then scoop it into bowls or cones, and enjoy your refreshing Lemon Sorbet!

This recipe creates a tangy and refreshing lemon sorbet that's perfect for cooling off on a hot day. You can also customize it by adding other citrus juices or experimenting with different flavors like mint or basil.

Pistachio Dairy-Free Ice Cream

Ingredients:

- 1 1/2 cups raw unsalted pistachios
- 2 cans (13.5 oz each) full-fat coconut milk, chilled overnight in the refrigerator
- 1/2 cup maple syrup or agave nectar
- 1 teaspoon vanilla extract
- Pinch of salt

Instructions:

1. Before you begin, make sure to place the cans of coconut milk in the refrigerator overnight to chill.
2. Preheat your oven to 350°F (175°C). Spread the pistachios in a single layer on a baking sheet and roast them in the preheated oven for 8-10 minutes, or until fragrant and lightly golden. Be careful not to let them burn. Remove from the oven and let them cool completely.
3. Once the pistachios are cooled, transfer them to a food processor or high-powered blender. Pulse or blend until finely ground, but be careful not to over-process them into a paste.
4. Once chilled, open the cans of coconut milk without shaking them. Scoop out the solid coconut cream that has risen to the top and transfer it to a mixing bowl. Reserve the coconut water for other uses or discard.
5. Add the ground pistachios, maple syrup or agave nectar, vanilla extract, and a pinch of salt to the coconut cream. Use a hand mixer or stand mixer to beat the mixture on medium-high speed until it becomes smooth and creamy, about 2-3 minutes.
6. Taste the mixture and adjust the sweetness to your liking, if necessary.
7. Transfer the mixture to an ice cream maker and churn according to the manufacturer's instructions until it reaches a soft-serve consistency.
8. If you prefer a firmer texture, transfer the churned ice cream to a freezer-safe container, cover it with a lid or plastic wrap, and freeze for at least 4-6 hours, or until firm.

9. Before serving, let the ice cream sit at room temperature for a few minutes to soften slightly. Then scoop it into bowls or cones, and enjoy your Pistachio Dairy-Free Ice Cream!

This recipe creates a creamy and nutty dairy-free ice cream with the rich flavor of pistachios. It's a delicious treat for pistachio lovers!

Chocolate Hazelnut Dairy-Free Ice Cream

Ingredients:

- 1 can (13.5 oz) full-fat coconut milk, chilled overnight in the refrigerator
- 1/2 cup creamy hazelnut butter (unsweetened)
- 1/4 cup cocoa powder (unsweetened)
- 1/3 cup maple syrup or agave nectar
- 1 teaspoon vanilla extract
- Pinch of salt
- Optional: chopped toasted hazelnuts for garnish

Instructions:

1. Before you begin, make sure to place the can of coconut milk in the refrigerator overnight to chill.
2. Once chilled, open the can of coconut milk without shaking it. Scoop out the solid coconut cream that has risen to the top and transfer it to a mixing bowl. Reserve the coconut water for other uses or discard.
3. Add the hazelnut butter, cocoa powder, maple syrup or agave nectar, vanilla extract, and a pinch of salt to the coconut cream. Use a hand mixer or stand mixer to beat the mixture on medium-high speed until it becomes smooth and creamy, about 2-3 minutes.
4. Taste the mixture and adjust the sweetness or cocoa flavor to your liking, if necessary.
5. Transfer the mixture to an ice cream maker and churn according to the manufacturer's instructions until it reaches a soft-serve consistency.
6. If you prefer a firmer texture, transfer the churned ice cream to a freezer-safe container, cover it with a lid or plastic wrap, and freeze for at least 4-6 hours, or until firm.
7. Before serving, let the ice cream sit at room temperature for a few minutes to soften slightly. Then scoop it into bowls or cones, sprinkle with chopped toasted hazelnuts if desired, and enjoy your Chocolate Hazelnut Dairy-Free Ice Cream!

This recipe creates a rich and creamy dairy-free ice cream with the irresistible combination of chocolate and hazelnut flavors. It's a decadent treat for chocolate lovers!

Pineapple Coconut Sorbet

Ingredients:

- 4 cups fresh pineapple chunks (about 1 medium pineapple)
- 1 can (13.5 oz) full-fat coconut milk, chilled overnight in the refrigerator
- 1/3 cup granulated sugar
- 2 tablespoons fresh lime juice
- Pinch of salt
- Optional: shredded coconut for garnish

Instructions:

1. Before you begin, make sure to place the can of coconut milk in the refrigerator overnight to chill.
2. In a blender or food processor, puree the fresh pineapple chunks until smooth.
3. Once chilled, open the can of coconut milk without shaking it. Scoop out the solid coconut cream that has risen to the top and transfer it to a mixing bowl. Reserve the coconut water for other uses or discard.
4. Add the pureed pineapple, granulated sugar, fresh lime juice, and a pinch of salt to the coconut cream. Use a hand mixer or stand mixer to beat the mixture on medium-high speed until it becomes smooth and creamy, about 2-3 minutes.
5. Taste the mixture and adjust the sweetness or lime flavor to your liking, if necessary.
6. Transfer the mixture to an ice cream maker and churn according to the manufacturer's instructions until it reaches a soft-serve consistency.
7. If you prefer a firmer texture, transfer the churned sorbet to a freezer-safe container, cover it with a lid or plastic wrap, and freeze for at least 4-6 hours, or until firm.
8. Before serving, let the sorbet sit at room temperature for a few minutes to soften slightly. Then scoop it into bowls or cones, sprinkle with shredded coconut if desired, and enjoy your Pineapple Coconut Sorbet!

This recipe creates a refreshing and tropical sorbet with the perfect balance of sweet pineapple and creamy coconut flavors. It's a delightful treat for hot summer days or any time you're craving something light and fruity!

Cherry Almond Dairy-Free Ice Cream

Ingredients:

- 2 cans (13.5 oz each) full-fat coconut milk, chilled overnight in the refrigerator
- 2 cups fresh or frozen cherries, pitted
- 1/2 cup maple syrup or agave nectar
- 1 teaspoon almond extract
- 1/4 cup sliced almonds, toasted (optional)
- Pinch of salt

Instructions:

1. Before you begin, make sure to place the cans of coconut milk in the refrigerator overnight to chill.
2. Once chilled, open the cans of coconut milk without shaking them. Scoop out the solid coconut cream that has risen to the top and transfer it to a mixing bowl. Reserve the coconut water for other uses or discard.
3. In a blender or food processor, puree the cherries until smooth.
4. Add the pureed cherries, maple syrup or agave nectar, almond extract, and a pinch of salt to the coconut cream. Use a hand mixer or stand mixer to beat the mixture on medium-high speed until it becomes smooth and creamy, about 2-3 minutes.
5. Taste the mixture and adjust the sweetness or almond flavor to your liking, if necessary.
6. If using, stir in the toasted sliced almonds for added texture and flavor.
7. Transfer the mixture to an ice cream maker and churn according to the manufacturer's instructions until it reaches a soft-serve consistency.
8. If you prefer a firmer texture, transfer the churned ice cream to a freezer-safe container, cover it with a lid or plastic wrap, and freeze for at least 4-6 hours, or until firm.
9. Before serving, let the ice cream sit at room temperature for a few minutes to soften slightly. Then scoop it into bowls or cones, and enjoy your Cherry Almond Dairy-Free Ice Cream!

This recipe creates a creamy and flavorful dairy-free ice cream with the natural sweetness of cherries and the nutty aroma of almond extract. It's a delightful treat for cherry almond lovers!

Matcha Green Tea Coconut Ice Cream

Ingredients:

- 2 cans (13.5 oz each) full-fat coconut milk, chilled overnight in the refrigerator
- 3 tablespoons matcha green tea powder
- 1/2 cup maple syrup or agave nectar
- 1 teaspoon vanilla extract
- Pinch of salt

Instructions:

1. Before you begin, make sure to place the cans of coconut milk in the refrigerator overnight to chill.
2. Once chilled, open the cans of coconut milk without shaking them. Scoop out the solid coconut cream that has risen to the top and transfer it to a mixing bowl. Reserve the coconut water for other uses or discard.
3. In a small bowl, whisk together the matcha green tea powder and a small amount of hot water until smooth to create a matcha paste.
4. Add the matcha paste, maple syrup or agave nectar, vanilla extract, and a pinch of salt to the coconut cream. Use a hand mixer or stand mixer to beat the mixture on medium-high speed until it becomes smooth and creamy, about 2-3 minutes.
5. Taste the mixture and adjust the sweetness or matcha flavor to your liking, if necessary.
6. Transfer the mixture to an ice cream maker and churn according to the manufacturer's instructions until it reaches a soft-serve consistency.
7. If you prefer a firmer texture, transfer the churned ice cream to a freezer-safe container, cover it with a lid or plastic wrap, and freeze for at least 4-6 hours, or until firm.
8. Before serving, let the ice cream sit at room temperature for a few minutes to soften slightly. Then scoop it into bowls or cones, and enjoy your Matcha Green Tea Coconut Ice Cream!

This recipe creates a creamy and vibrant dairy-free ice cream with the distinctive flavor of matcha green tea combined with the richness of coconut milk. It's a refreshing and delicious treat for matcha enthusiasts!

Blackberry Coconut Milk Ice Cream

Ingredients:

- 2 cans (13.5 oz each) full-fat coconut milk, chilled overnight in the refrigerator
- 2 cups fresh or frozen blackberries
- 1/2 cup maple syrup or agave nectar
- 1 teaspoon vanilla extract
- Pinch of salt

Instructions:

1. Before you begin, make sure to place the cans of coconut milk in the refrigerator overnight to chill.
2. In a blender or food processor, puree the blackberries until smooth. Strain the puree through a fine-mesh sieve to remove the seeds if desired. Set aside.
3. Once chilled, open the cans of coconut milk without shaking them. Scoop out the solid coconut cream that has risen to the top and transfer it to a mixing bowl. Reserve the coconut water for other uses or discard.
4. Add the blackberry puree, maple syrup or agave nectar, vanilla extract, and a pinch of salt to the coconut cream. Use a hand mixer or stand mixer to beat the mixture on medium-high speed until it becomes smooth and creamy, about 2-3 minutes.
5. Taste the mixture and adjust the sweetness to your liking, if necessary.
6. Transfer the mixture to an ice cream maker and churn according to the manufacturer's instructions until it reaches a soft-serve consistency.
7. If you prefer a firmer texture, transfer the churned ice cream to a freezer-safe container, cover it with a lid or plastic wrap, and freeze for at least 4-6 hours, or until firm.
8. Before serving, let the ice cream sit at room temperature for a few minutes to soften slightly. Then scoop it into bowls or cones, and enjoy your Blackberry Coconut Milk Ice Cream!

This recipe creates a creamy and fruity dairy-free ice cream with the sweet-tart flavor of blackberries combined with the richness of coconut milk. It's a delicious and refreshing treat for any time of year!

Mocha Almond Fudge Dairy-Free Ice Cream

Ingredients:

For the ice cream base:

- 2 cans (13.5 oz each) full-fat coconut milk, chilled overnight in the refrigerator
- 1/4 cup cocoa powder (unsweetened)
- 1/4 cup strong brewed coffee or espresso, cooled
- 1/2 cup maple syrup or agave nectar
- 1 teaspoon vanilla extract
- Pinch of salt

For the almond fudge swirl:

- 1/4 cup almond butter (unsweetened)
- 2 tablespoons cocoa powder (unsweetened)
- 2 tablespoons maple syrup or agave nectar
- 2 tablespoons coconut oil, melted
- 1/4 teaspoon vanilla extract
- 1/4 cup chopped almonds, toasted (optional)

Instructions:

1. Before you begin, make sure to place the cans of coconut milk in the refrigerator overnight to chill.
2. In a small bowl, whisk together the cocoa powder and brewed coffee until smooth. Set aside.
3. Once chilled, open the cans of coconut milk without shaking them. Scoop out the solid coconut cream that has risen to the top and transfer it to a mixing bowl. Reserve the coconut water for other uses or discard.
4. Add the cocoa-coffee mixture, maple syrup or agave nectar, vanilla extract, and a pinch of salt to the coconut cream. Use a hand mixer or stand mixer to beat the

mixture on medium-high speed until it becomes smooth and creamy, about 2-3 minutes.
5. Taste the mixture and adjust the sweetness or cocoa-coffee flavor to your liking, if necessary.
6. For the almond fudge swirl, in a separate bowl, whisk together the almond butter, cocoa powder, maple syrup or agave nectar, melted coconut oil, and vanilla extract until smooth.
7. If using, stir in the chopped toasted almonds for added texture.
8. Transfer half of the ice cream mixture to a freezer-safe container. Spoon half of the almond fudge mixture over the ice cream. Repeat with the remaining ice cream and almond fudge, creating swirls with a spoon or knife.
9. Cover the container with a lid or plastic wrap and freeze for at least 4-6 hours, or until firm.
10. Before serving, let the ice cream sit at room temperature for a few minutes to soften slightly. Then scoop it into bowls or cones, and enjoy your Mocha Almond Fudge Dairy-Free Ice Cream!

This recipe creates a rich and indulgent dairy-free ice cream with the bold flavors of mocha and almond fudge. It's a perfect treat for coffee and chocolate lovers alike!

Peach Sorbet

Ingredients:

- 4 cups ripe peaches, peeled, pitted, and chopped
- 1/2 cup granulated sugar
- 1/4 cup water
- 1 tablespoon lemon juice
- Pinch of salt

Instructions:

1. In a small saucepan, combine the granulated sugar, water, lemon juice, and a pinch of salt. Heat over medium heat, stirring occasionally, until the sugar is completely dissolved. This will create a simple syrup.
2. Once the sugar is dissolved, remove the saucepan from the heat and let the simple syrup cool to room temperature.
3. In a blender or food processor, puree the chopped peaches until smooth.
4. Once the simple syrup is cooled, add it to the peach puree and blend until well combined.
5. Taste the mixture and adjust the sweetness or tartness by adding more sugar or lemon juice if necessary.
6. Pour the peach mixture into a shallow dish or baking pan and place it in the freezer.
7. After about an hour, check the mixture. It should start to freeze around the edges. Use a fork to scrape the frozen edges and mix them into the liquid center.
8. Continue to check and stir the mixture every 30 minutes to an hour until it is completely frozen and has a smooth, sorbet-like texture. This process usually takes about 3-4 hours.
9. Once the sorbet is frozen to your desired consistency, transfer it to an airtight container and store it in the freezer until ready to serve.
10. Before serving, let the sorbet sit at room temperature for a few minutes to soften slightly. Then scoop it into bowls or cones, and enjoy your refreshing Peach Sorbet!

This recipe creates a delightful and refreshing sorbet with the natural sweetness of ripe peaches. It's perfect for hot summer days or anytime you're craving a light and fruity dessert!

Cookies and Cream Dairy-Free Ice Cream

Ingredients:

- 2 cans (13.5 oz each) full-fat coconut milk, chilled overnight in the refrigerator
- 1/2 cup maple syrup or agave nectar
- 1 teaspoon vanilla extract
- Pinch of salt
- 10-12 dairy-free chocolate sandwich cookies (such as Oreos), crushed

Instructions:

1. Before you begin, make sure to place the cans of coconut milk in the refrigerator overnight to chill.
2. Once chilled, open the cans of coconut milk without shaking them. Scoop out the solid coconut cream that has risen to the top and transfer it to a mixing bowl. Reserve the coconut water for other uses or discard.
3. Add the maple syrup or agave nectar, vanilla extract, and a pinch of salt to the coconut cream. Use a hand mixer or stand mixer to beat the mixture on medium-high speed until it becomes smooth and creamy, about 2-3 minutes.
4. Taste the mixture and adjust the sweetness or vanilla flavor to your liking, if necessary.
5. Crush the dairy-free chocolate sandwich cookies into small pieces. You can do this by placing them in a plastic bag and using a rolling pin to crush them, or by pulsing them in a food processor.
6. Gently fold the crushed cookies into the coconut milk mixture until evenly distributed.
7. Transfer the mixture to an ice cream maker and churn according to the manufacturer's instructions until it reaches a soft-serve consistency.
8. If you prefer a firmer texture, transfer the churned ice cream to a freezer-safe container, cover it with a lid or plastic wrap, and freeze for at least 4-6 hours, or until firm.
9. Before serving, let the ice cream sit at room temperature for a few minutes to soften slightly. Then scoop it into bowls or cones, and enjoy your Cookies and Cream Dairy-Free Ice Cream!

This recipe creates a creamy and indulgent dairy-free ice cream with the classic combination of chocolate sandwich cookies and vanilla flavor. It's a delicious treat for anyone looking for a dairy-free alternative to traditional cookies and cream ice cream!

Raspberry Sorbet

Ingredients:

- 4 cups fresh or frozen raspberries
- 1 cup granulated sugar
- 1 cup water
- 2 tablespoons freshly squeezed lemon juice

Instructions:

1. In a small saucepan, combine the granulated sugar and water. Heat over medium heat, stirring occasionally, until the sugar is completely dissolved. This will create a simple syrup.
2. Once the sugar is dissolved, remove the saucepan from the heat and let the simple syrup cool to room temperature.
3. In a blender or food processor, puree the raspberries until smooth.
4. Pour the raspberry puree through a fine-mesh sieve into a large bowl to remove the seeds. Press on the solids with a spoon to extract as much liquid as possible.
5. Stir the cooled simple syrup and lemon juice into the raspberry puree until well combined.
6. Taste the mixture and adjust the sweetness or tartness by adding more sugar or lemon juice if necessary.
7. Pour the raspberry mixture into an ice cream maker and churn according to the manufacturer's instructions until it reaches a soft-serve consistency.
8. If you prefer a firmer texture, transfer the churned sorbet to a freezer-safe container, cover it with a lid or plastic wrap, and freeze for at least 4-6 hours, or until firm.
9. Before serving, let the sorbet sit at room temperature for a few minutes to soften slightly. Then scoop it into bowls or cones, and enjoy your refreshing Raspberry Sorbet!

This recipe creates a vibrant and refreshing sorbet with the natural sweetness and tartness of raspberries. It's perfect for hot summer days or anytime you're craving a light and fruity dessert!

Chocolate Peanut Butter Dairy-Free Ice Cream

Ingredients:

- 2 cans (13.5 oz each) full-fat coconut milk, chilled overnight in the refrigerator
- 1/2 cup cocoa powder (unsweetened)
- 1/2 cup creamy peanut butter (unsweetened)
- 1/2 cup maple syrup or agave nectar
- 1 teaspoon vanilla extract
- Pinch of salt
- Optional: chopped peanuts for garnish

Instructions:

1. Before you begin, make sure to place the cans of coconut milk in the refrigerator overnight to chill.
2. Once chilled, open the cans of coconut milk without shaking them. Scoop out the solid coconut cream that has risen to the top and transfer it to a mixing bowl. Reserve the coconut water for other uses or discard.
3. In a separate microwave-safe bowl, heat the peanut butter until it's softened and easier to work with, about 30-60 seconds.
4. Add the softened peanut butter, cocoa powder, maple syrup or agave nectar, vanilla extract, and a pinch of salt to the coconut cream. Use a hand mixer or stand mixer to beat the mixture on medium-high speed until it becomes smooth and creamy, about 2-3 minutes.
5. Taste the mixture and adjust the sweetness or cocoa flavor to your liking, if necessary.
6. Transfer the mixture to an ice cream maker and churn according to the manufacturer's instructions until it reaches a soft-serve consistency.
7. If you prefer a firmer texture, transfer the churned ice cream to a freezer-safe container, cover it with a lid or plastic wrap, and freeze for at least 4-6 hours, or until firm.
8. Before serving, let the ice cream sit at room temperature for a few minutes to soften slightly. Then scoop it into bowls or cones, sprinkle with chopped peanuts if desired, and enjoy your Chocolate Peanut Butter Dairy-Free Ice Cream!

This recipe creates a rich and creamy dairy-free ice cream with the irresistible combination of chocolate and peanut butter flavors. It's a decadent treat for peanut butter lovers!

Coconut Lime Dairy-Free Ice Cream

Ingredients:

- 2 cans (13.5 oz each) full-fat coconut milk, chilled overnight in the refrigerator
- 1/2 cup maple syrup or agave nectar
- Zest of 2 limes
- 1/4 cup freshly squeezed lime juice (about 2-3 limes)
- 1 teaspoon vanilla extract
- Pinch of salt
- Optional: shredded coconut for garnish

Instructions:

1. Before you begin, make sure to place the cans of coconut milk in the refrigerator overnight to chill.
2. Once chilled, open the cans of coconut milk without shaking them. Scoop out the solid coconut cream that has risen to the top and transfer it to a mixing bowl. Reserve the coconut water for other uses or discard.
3. Add the maple syrup or agave nectar, lime zest, lime juice, vanilla extract, and a pinch of salt to the coconut cream. Use a hand mixer or stand mixer to beat the mixture on medium-high speed until it becomes smooth and creamy, about 2-3 minutes.
4. Taste the mixture and adjust the sweetness or lime flavor to your liking, if necessary.
5. Transfer the mixture to an ice cream maker and churn according to the manufacturer's instructions until it reaches a soft-serve consistency.
6. If you prefer a firmer texture, transfer the churned ice cream to a freezer-safe container, cover it with a lid or plastic wrap, and freeze for at least 4-6 hours, or until firm.
7. Before serving, let the ice cream sit at room temperature for a few minutes to soften slightly. Then scoop it into bowls or cones, sprinkle with shredded coconut if desired, and enjoy your Coconut Lime Dairy-Free Ice Cream!

This recipe creates a refreshing and tropical dairy-free ice cream with the bright and zesty flavors of lime combined with the creaminess of coconut milk. It's a perfect treat for hot summer days or anytime you're craving a light and citrusy dessert!

Maple Walnut Dairy-Free Ice Cream

Ingredients:

- 2 cans (13.5 oz each) full-fat coconut milk, chilled overnight in the refrigerator
- 1/2 cup maple syrup
- 1 teaspoon vanilla extract
- 1/2 cup chopped walnuts

Instructions:

1. Before you begin, make sure to place the cans of coconut milk in the refrigerator overnight to chill.
2. Once chilled, open the cans of coconut milk without shaking them. Scoop out the solid coconut cream that has risen to the top and transfer it to a mixing bowl. Reserve the coconut water for other uses or discard.
3. Add the maple syrup and vanilla extract to the coconut cream. Use a hand mixer or stand mixer to beat the mixture on medium-high speed until it becomes smooth and creamy, about 2-3 minutes.
4. Stir in the chopped walnuts until evenly distributed throughout the mixture.
5. Transfer the mixture to an ice cream maker and churn according to the manufacturer's instructions until it reaches a soft-serve consistency.
6. If you prefer a firmer texture, transfer the churned ice cream to a freezer-safe container, cover it with a lid or plastic wrap, and freeze for at least 4-6 hours, or until firm.
7. Before serving, let the ice cream sit at room temperature for a few minutes to soften slightly. Then scoop it into bowls or cones, and enjoy your Maple Walnut Dairy-Free Ice Cream!

This recipe creates a creamy and flavorful dairy-free ice cream with the rich taste of maple syrup and the crunch of walnuts. It's a delicious treat for maple walnut lovers!

Orange Creamsicle Dairy-Free Ice Cream

Ingredients:

- 2 cans (13.5 oz each) full-fat coconut milk, chilled overnight in the refrigerator
- 1/2 cup freshly squeezed orange juice (about 2-3 oranges)
- Zest of 1 orange
- 1/3 cup maple syrup or agave nectar
- 1 teaspoon vanilla extract
- Pinch of salt

Instructions:

1. Before you begin, make sure to place the cans of coconut milk in the refrigerator overnight to chill.
2. Once chilled, open the cans of coconut milk without shaking them. Scoop out the solid coconut cream that has risen to the top and transfer it to a mixing bowl. Reserve the coconut water for other uses or discard.
3. Add the freshly squeezed orange juice, orange zest, maple syrup or agave nectar, vanilla extract, and a pinch of salt to the coconut cream. Use a hand mixer or stand mixer to beat the mixture on medium-high speed until it becomes smooth and creamy, about 2-3 minutes.
4. Taste the mixture and adjust the sweetness or orange flavor to your liking, if necessary.
5. Transfer the mixture to an ice cream maker and churn according to the manufacturer's instructions until it reaches a soft-serve consistency.
6. If you prefer a firmer texture, transfer the churned ice cream to a freezer-safe container, cover it with a lid or plastic wrap, and freeze for at least 4-6 hours, or until firm.
7. Before serving, let the ice cream sit at room temperature for a few minutes to soften slightly. Then scoop it into bowls or cones, and enjoy your Orange Creamsicle Dairy-Free Ice Cream!

This recipe creates a creamy and refreshing dairy-free ice cream with the bright and citrusy flavors of orange. It's reminiscent of the classic creamsicle treat, but with a dairy-free twist!

Blueberry Banana Coconut Milk Ice Cream

Ingredients:

- 2 cans (13.5 oz each) full-fat coconut milk, chilled overnight in the refrigerator
- 2 ripe bananas, peeled and sliced
- 1 cup fresh or frozen blueberries
- 1/3 cup maple syrup or agave nectar
- 1 teaspoon vanilla extract
- Pinch of salt

Instructions:

1. Before you begin, make sure to place the cans of coconut milk in the refrigerator overnight to chill.
2. Once chilled, open the cans of coconut milk without shaking them. Scoop out the solid coconut cream that has risen to the top and transfer it to a mixing bowl. Reserve the coconut water for other uses or discard.
3. In a blender or food processor, combine the sliced bananas, blueberries, maple syrup or agave nectar, vanilla extract, and a pinch of salt. Blend until smooth.
4. Add the banana-blueberry mixture to the coconut cream. Use a hand mixer or stand mixer to beat the mixture on medium-high speed until it becomes smooth and creamy, about 2-3 minutes.
5. Taste the mixture and adjust the sweetness or vanilla flavor to your liking, if necessary.
6. Transfer the mixture to an ice cream maker and churn according to the manufacturer's instructions until it reaches a soft-serve consistency.
7. If you prefer a firmer texture, transfer the churned ice cream to a freezer-safe container, cover it with a lid or plastic wrap, and freeze for at least 4-6 hours, or until firm.
8. Before serving, let the ice cream sit at room temperature for a few minutes to soften slightly. Then scoop it into bowls or cones, and enjoy your Blueberry Banana Coconut Milk Ice Cream!

This recipe creates a creamy and fruity dairy-free ice cream with the natural sweetness of bananas and blueberries combined with the richness of coconut milk. It's a delicious and refreshing treat for any time of year!

Vegan Rocky Road Ice Cream

Ingredients:

- 2 cans (13.5 oz each) full-fat coconut milk, chilled overnight in the refrigerator
- 1/3 cup cocoa powder (unsweetened)
- 1/2 cup maple syrup or agave nectar
- 1 teaspoon vanilla extract
- Pinch of salt
- 1/2 cup vegan chocolate chips
- 1/2 cup chopped toasted almonds
- 1/2 cup mini vegan marshmallows

Instructions:

1. Before you begin, make sure to place the cans of coconut milk in the refrigerator overnight to chill.
2. Once chilled, open the cans of coconut milk without shaking them. Scoop out the solid coconut cream that has risen to the top and transfer it to a mixing bowl. Reserve the coconut water for other uses or discard.
3. Add the cocoa powder, maple syrup or agave nectar, vanilla extract, and a pinch of salt to the coconut cream. Use a hand mixer or stand mixer to beat the mixture on medium-high speed until it becomes smooth and creamy, about 2-3 minutes.
4. Taste the mixture and adjust the sweetness or cocoa flavor to your liking, if necessary.
5. Stir in the vegan chocolate chips, chopped toasted almonds, and mini vegan marshmallows until evenly distributed throughout the mixture.
6. Transfer the mixture to an ice cream maker and churn according to the manufacturer's instructions until it reaches a soft-serve consistency.
7. If you prefer a firmer texture, transfer the churned ice cream to a freezer-safe container, cover it with a lid or plastic wrap, and freeze for at least 4-6 hours, or until firm.
8. Before serving, let the ice cream sit at room temperature for a few minutes to soften slightly. Then scoop it into bowls or cones, and enjoy your Vegan Rocky Road Ice Cream!

This recipe creates a rich and indulgent vegan ice cream with the classic combination of chocolate, almonds, and marshmallows. It's a delicious treat for anyone looking for a dairy-free alternative to traditional rocky road ice cream!

Pumpkin Spice Dairy-Free Ice Cream

Ingredients:

- 1 can (13.5 oz) full-fat coconut milk, chilled overnight in the refrigerator
- 1 cup pumpkin puree (canned or homemade)
- 1/2 cup maple syrup or agave nectar
- 1 teaspoon vanilla extract
- 1 teaspoon ground cinnamon
- 1/2 teaspoon ground ginger
- 1/4 teaspoon ground nutmeg
- 1/4 teaspoon ground cloves
- Pinch of salt

Instructions:

1. Before you begin, make sure to place the can of coconut milk in the refrigerator overnight to chill.
2. Once chilled, open the can of coconut milk without shaking it. Scoop out the solid coconut cream that has risen to the top and transfer it to a mixing bowl. Reserve the coconut water for other uses or discard.
3. Add the pumpkin puree, maple syrup or agave nectar, vanilla extract, ground cinnamon, ground ginger, ground nutmeg, ground cloves, and a pinch of salt to the coconut cream. Use a hand mixer or stand mixer to beat the mixture on medium-high speed until it becomes smooth and creamy, about 2-3 minutes.
4. Taste the mixture and adjust the sweetness or pumpkin spice flavor to your liking, if necessary.
5. Transfer the mixture to an ice cream maker and churn according to the manufacturer's instructions until it reaches a soft-serve consistency.
6. If you prefer a firmer texture, transfer the churned ice cream to a freezer-safe container, cover it with a lid or plastic wrap, and freeze for at least 4-6 hours, or until firm.

7. Before serving, let the ice cream sit at room temperature for a few minutes to soften slightly. Then scoop it into bowls or cones, and enjoy your Pumpkin Spice Dairy-Free Ice Cream!

This recipe creates a creamy and flavorful dairy-free ice cream with the warm and comforting flavors of pumpkin spice. It's a perfect treat for the fall season or anytime you're craving a taste of autumn!

Chocolate Chip Cookie Dough Coconut Ice Cream

Ingredients:

For the cookie dough:

- 1/2 cup vegan butter, softened
- 1/4 cup brown sugar
- 1/4 cup granulated sugar
- 1 teaspoon vanilla extract
- 1 cup all-purpose flour
- 1/2 cup dairy-free chocolate chips

For the ice cream base:

- 2 cans (13.5 oz each) full-fat coconut milk, chilled overnight in the refrigerator
- 1/2 cup maple syrup or agave nectar
- 1 teaspoon vanilla extract
- Pinch of salt

Instructions:

1. Start by making the cookie dough. In a mixing bowl, cream together the vegan butter, brown sugar, granulated sugar, and vanilla extract until smooth and creamy.
2. Gradually add the flour to the butter mixture, mixing until well combined and a dough forms. Fold in the dairy-free chocolate chips.
3. Roll the cookie dough into small balls, about 1 teaspoon each, and place them on a baking sheet lined with parchment paper. Place the baking sheet in the freezer and freeze the cookie dough balls until firm, about 30 minutes to 1 hour.
4. While the cookie dough is chilling, prepare the ice cream base. Open the cans of coconut milk without shaking them. Scoop out the solid coconut cream that has

risen to the top and transfer it to a mixing bowl. Reserve the coconut water for other uses or discard.

5. Add the maple syrup or agave nectar, vanilla extract, and a pinch of salt to the coconut cream. Use a hand mixer or stand mixer to beat the mixture on medium-high speed until it becomes smooth and creamy, about 2-3 minutes.
6. Once the cookie dough balls are firm, remove them from the freezer. Gently fold them into the coconut milk mixture until evenly distributed.
7. Transfer the mixture to an ice cream maker and churn according to the manufacturer's instructions until it reaches a soft-serve consistency.
8. If you prefer a firmer texture, transfer the churned ice cream to a freezer-safe container, cover it with a lid or plastic wrap, and freeze for at least 4-6 hours, or until firm.
9. Before serving, let the ice cream sit at room temperature for a few minutes to soften slightly. Then scoop it into bowls or cones, and enjoy your Chocolate Chip Cookie Dough Coconut Ice Cream!

This recipe combines creamy coconut milk ice cream with chunks of cookie dough for a delicious and indulgent treat that's perfect for any occasion!

Strawberry Rhubarb Dairy-Free Ice Cream

Ingredients:

For the strawberry rhubarb compote:

- 2 cups chopped rhubarb
- 2 cups chopped strawberries
- 1/2 cup granulated sugar
- 1 tablespoon lemon juice

For the ice cream base:

- 2 cans (13.5 oz each) full-fat coconut milk, chilled overnight in the refrigerator
- 1/3 cup maple syrup or agave nectar
- 1 teaspoon vanilla extract
- Pinch of salt

Instructions:

1. Start by making the strawberry rhubarb compote. In a medium saucepan, combine the chopped rhubarb, chopped strawberries, granulated sugar, and lemon juice. Cook over medium heat, stirring occasionally, until the fruit is soft and the mixture has thickened, about 10-15 minutes. Remove from heat and let cool completely.
2. Once the compote is cooled, prepare the ice cream base. Open the cans of coconut milk without shaking them. Scoop out the solid coconut cream that has risen to the top and transfer it to a mixing bowl. Reserve the coconut water for other uses or discard.
3. Add the maple syrup or agave nectar, vanilla extract, and a pinch of salt to the coconut cream. Use a hand mixer or stand mixer to beat the mixture on medium-high speed until it becomes smooth and creamy, about 2-3 minutes.
4. Gently fold the cooled strawberry rhubarb compote into the coconut milk mixture until evenly distributed.

5. Transfer the mixture to an ice cream maker and churn according to the manufacturer's instructions until it reaches a soft-serve consistency.
6. If you prefer a firmer texture, transfer the churned ice cream to a freezer-safe container, cover it with a lid or plastic wrap, and freeze for at least 4-6 hours, or until firm.
7. Before serving, let the ice cream sit at room temperature for a few minutes to soften slightly. Then scoop it into bowls or cones, and enjoy your Strawberry Rhubarb Dairy-Free Ice Cream!

This recipe combines the sweet-tart flavors of strawberries and rhubarb with creamy coconut milk for a refreshing and dairy-free dessert that's perfect for enjoying during the warmer months!

Coconut Mango Dairy-Free Ice Cream

Ingredients:

- 2 cans (13.5 oz each) full-fat coconut milk, chilled overnight in the refrigerator
- 2 ripe mangoes, peeled, pitted, and chopped
- 1/2 cup maple syrup or agave nectar
- 1 teaspoon vanilla extract
- Pinch of salt

Instructions:

1. Before you begin, make sure to place the cans of coconut milk in the refrigerator overnight to chill.
2. Once chilled, open the cans of coconut milk without shaking them. Scoop out the solid coconut cream that has risen to the top and transfer it to a mixing bowl. Reserve the coconut water for other uses or discard.
3. In a blender or food processor, puree the chopped mangoes until smooth.
4. Add the mango puree, maple syrup or agave nectar, vanilla extract, and a pinch of salt to the coconut cream. Use a hand mixer or stand mixer to beat the mixture on medium-high speed until it becomes smooth and creamy, about 2-3 minutes.
5. Taste the mixture and adjust the sweetness or vanilla flavor to your liking, if necessary.
6. Transfer the mixture to an ice cream maker and churn according to the manufacturer's instructions until it reaches a soft-serve consistency.
7. If you prefer a firmer texture, transfer the churned ice cream to a freezer-safe container, cover it with a lid or plastic wrap, and freeze for at least 4-6 hours, or until firm.
8. Before serving, let the ice cream sit at room temperature for a few minutes to soften slightly. Then scoop it into bowls or cones, and enjoy your Coconut Mango Dairy-Free Ice Cream!

This recipe creates a creamy and tropical dairy-free ice cream with the natural sweetness and tanginess of ripe mangoes combined with the richness of coconut milk. It's a perfect treat for hot summer days or anytime you're craving a taste of the tropics!

Salted Caramel Chocolate Dairy-Free Ice Cream

Ingredients:

For the salted caramel sauce:

- 1 cup coconut cream (from a can of chilled full-fat coconut milk)
- 1 cup brown sugar
- 2 tablespoons coconut oil
- 1 teaspoon vanilla extract
- 1 teaspoon sea salt

For the chocolate ice cream base:

- 2 cans (13.5 oz each) full-fat coconut milk, chilled overnight in the refrigerator
- 1/2 cup cocoa powder (unsweetened)
- 1/3 cup maple syrup or agave nectar
- 1 teaspoon vanilla extract
- Pinch of salt

Instructions:

Salted Caramel Sauce:

1. In a saucepan, combine the coconut cream, brown sugar, and coconut oil over medium heat.
2. Stir continuously until the sugar has dissolved and the mixture comes to a gentle boil.
3. Reduce the heat to low and simmer for 5-7 minutes, stirring occasionally, until the sauce has thickened.
4. Remove from heat and stir in the vanilla extract and sea salt. Let the caramel sauce cool completely.

Chocolate Ice Cream Base:

1. Before you begin, make sure to place the cans of coconut milk in the refrigerator overnight to chill.
2. Once chilled, open the cans of coconut milk without shaking them. Scoop out the solid coconut cream that has risen to the top and transfer it to a mixing bowl. Reserve the coconut water for other uses or discard.
3. Add the cocoa powder, maple syrup or agave nectar, vanilla extract, and a pinch of salt to the coconut cream. Use a hand mixer or stand mixer to beat the mixture on medium-high speed until it becomes smooth and creamy, about 2-3 minutes.
4. Taste the mixture and adjust the sweetness or cocoa flavor to your liking, if necessary.
5. Gently fold in 1/2 cup of the cooled salted caramel sauce into the chocolate coconut milk mixture until evenly distributed.
6. Transfer the mixture to an ice cream maker and churn according to the manufacturer's instructions until it reaches a soft-serve consistency.
7. If you prefer a firmer texture, transfer the churned ice cream to a freezer-safe container, cover it with a lid or plastic wrap, and freeze for at least 4-6 hours, or until firm.
8. Before serving, let the ice cream sit at room temperature for a few minutes to soften slightly. Then scoop it into bowls or cones, drizzle with additional salted caramel sauce if desired, and enjoy your Salted Caramel Chocolate Dairy-Free Ice Cream!

This recipe combines rich chocolate coconut milk ice cream with swirls of homemade salted caramel sauce for a decadent and indulgent dairy-free treat!

Kiwi Sorbet

Ingredients:

- 6-8 ripe kiwis
- 1/2 cup granulated sugar (adjust to taste, depending on the sweetness of the kiwis)
- 1/4 cup water
- 1-2 tablespoons freshly squeezed lemon juice (optional, to enhance the flavor)

Instructions:

1. Peel the kiwis and cut them into small chunks. Remove any seeds if present.
2. Place the kiwi chunks in a blender or food processor and blend until smooth. You should have about 2 cups of puree.
3. In a small saucepan, combine the granulated sugar and water. Heat over medium heat, stirring occasionally, until the sugar is completely dissolved. This will create a simple syrup.
4. Remove the simple syrup from the heat and let it cool to room temperature.
5. Once the simple syrup is cooled, add it to the kiwi puree and stir to combine. Add freshly squeezed lemon juice to taste, if desired, to enhance the flavor of the sorbet.
6. Transfer the kiwi mixture to an ice cream maker and churn according to the manufacturer's instructions until it reaches a soft-serve consistency.
7. If you prefer a firmer texture, transfer the churned sorbet to a freezer-safe container, cover it with a lid or plastic wrap, and freeze for at least 4-6 hours, or until firm.
8. Before serving, let the sorbet sit at room temperature for a few minutes to soften slightly. Then scoop it into bowls or cones, and enjoy your refreshing Kiwi Sorbet!

This recipe creates a vibrant and refreshing sorbet with the natural sweetness and tanginess of ripe kiwis. It's perfect for hot summer days or anytime you're craving a light and fruity dessert!

Cherry Chocolate Chip Dairy-Free Ice Cream

Ingredients:

- 2 cans (13.5 oz each) full-fat coconut milk, chilled overnight in the refrigerator
- 2 cups pitted cherries (fresh or frozen)
- 1/2 cup maple syrup or agave nectar
- 1 teaspoon vanilla extract
- Pinch of salt
- 1/2 cup dairy-free chocolate chips

Instructions:

1. Before you begin, make sure to place the cans of coconut milk in the refrigerator overnight to chill.
2. Once chilled, open the cans of coconut milk without shaking them. Scoop out the solid coconut cream that has risen to the top and transfer it to a mixing bowl. Reserve the coconut water for other uses or discard.
3. In a blender or food processor, puree the pitted cherries until smooth.
4. Add the cherry puree, maple syrup or agave nectar, vanilla extract, and a pinch of salt to the coconut cream. Use a hand mixer or stand mixer to beat the mixture on medium-high speed until it becomes smooth and creamy, about 2-3 minutes.
5. Taste the mixture and adjust the sweetness or vanilla flavor to your liking, if necessary.
6. Gently fold in the dairy-free chocolate chips until evenly distributed throughout the mixture.
7. Transfer the mixture to an ice cream maker and churn according to the manufacturer's instructions until it reaches a soft-serve consistency.
8. If you prefer a firmer texture, transfer the churned ice cream to a freezer-safe container, cover it with a lid or plastic wrap, and freeze for at least 4-6 hours, or until firm.
9. Before serving, let the ice cream sit at room temperature for a few minutes to soften slightly. Then scoop it into bowls or cones, and enjoy your Cherry Chocolate Chip Dairy-Free Ice Cream!

This recipe combines the natural sweetness of cherries with the richness of coconut milk and the indulgence of dairy-free chocolate chips for a delicious frozen treat that everyone can enjoy!

Pineapple Basil Dairy-Free Ice Cream

Ingredients:

- 2 cans (13.5 oz each) full-fat coconut milk, chilled overnight in the refrigerator
- 2 cups fresh pineapple chunks
- 1/2 cup maple syrup or agave nectar
- 1/4 cup fresh basil leaves, packed
- 1 teaspoon vanilla extract
- Pinch of salt

Instructions:

1. Before you begin, make sure to place the cans of coconut milk in the refrigerator overnight to chill.
2. Once chilled, open the cans of coconut milk without shaking them. Scoop out the solid coconut cream that has risen to the top and transfer it to a mixing bowl. Reserve the coconut water for other uses or discard.
3. In a blender or food processor, combine the fresh pineapple chunks and basil leaves. Blend until smooth.
4. Add the pineapple-basil puree, maple syrup or agave nectar, vanilla extract, and a pinch of salt to the coconut cream. Use a hand mixer or stand mixer to beat the mixture on medium-high speed until it becomes smooth and creamy, about 2-3 minutes.
5. Taste the mixture and adjust the sweetness or basil flavor to your liking, if necessary.
6. Transfer the mixture to an ice cream maker and churn according to the manufacturer's instructions until it reaches a soft-serve consistency.
7. If you prefer a firmer texture, transfer the churned ice cream to a freezer-safe container, cover it with a lid or plastic wrap, and freeze for at least 4-6 hours, or until firm.
8. Before serving, let the ice cream sit at room temperature for a few minutes to soften slightly. Then scoop it into bowls or cones, and enjoy your Pineapple Basil Dairy-Free Ice Cream!

This recipe combines the tropical sweetness of pineapple with the fresh, herbal notes of basil for a unique and refreshing dairy-free ice cream that's perfect for summer!

Raspberry Coconut Milk Ice Cream

Ingredients:

- 2 cans (13.5 oz each) full-fat coconut milk, chilled overnight in the refrigerator
- 2 cups fresh or frozen raspberries
- 1/2 cup maple syrup or agave nectar
- 1 teaspoon vanilla extract
- Pinch of salt

Instructions:

1. Before you begin, make sure to place the cans of coconut milk in the refrigerator overnight to chill.
2. Once chilled, open the cans of coconut milk without shaking them. Scoop out the solid coconut cream that has risen to the top and transfer it to a mixing bowl. Reserve the coconut water for other uses or discard.
3. In a blender or food processor, puree the raspberries until smooth.
4. Add the raspberry puree, maple syrup or agave nectar, vanilla extract, and a pinch of salt to the coconut cream. Use a hand mixer or stand mixer to beat the mixture on medium-high speed until it becomes smooth and creamy, about 2-3 minutes.
5. Taste the mixture and adjust the sweetness to your liking, if necessary.
6. Transfer the mixture to an ice cream maker and churn according to the manufacturer's instructions until it reaches a soft-serve consistency.
7. If you prefer a firmer texture, transfer the churned ice cream to a freezer-safe container, cover it with a lid or plastic wrap, and freeze for at least 4-6 hours, or until firm.
8. Before serving, let the ice cream sit at room temperature for a few minutes to soften slightly. Then scoop it into bowls or cones, and enjoy your Raspberry Coconut Milk Ice Cream!

This recipe creates a creamy and refreshing dairy-free ice cream with the bright and tangy flavors of fresh raspberries combined with the richness of coconut milk. It's a perfect treat for hot summer days or anytime you're craving a fruity dessert!

Vegan Butter Pecan Ice Cream

Ingredients:

For the pecans:

- 1 cup pecan halves
- 1 tablespoon vegan butter
- 1 tablespoon maple syrup

For the ice cream base:

- 2 cans (13.5 oz each) full-fat coconut milk, chilled overnight in the refrigerator
- 1/2 cup brown sugar (or coconut sugar)
- 1 tablespoon cornstarch
- 1 teaspoon vanilla extract
- Pinch of salt

Instructions:

For the pecans:

1. Preheat your oven to 350°F (175°C).
2. In a small saucepan, melt the vegan butter over medium heat. Add the maple syrup and pecans, stirring until the pecans are evenly coated.
3. Spread the coated pecans onto a baking sheet lined with parchment paper in a single layer.
4. Bake for 8-10 minutes, or until the pecans are fragrant and lightly toasted. Keep an eye on them to prevent burning. Once done, remove from the oven and let them cool completely. Once cooled, chop the pecans into smaller pieces.

For the ice cream base:

1. Before you begin, make sure to place the cans of coconut milk in the refrigerator overnight to chill.
2. Once chilled, open the cans of coconut milk without shaking them. Scoop out the solid coconut cream that has risen to the top and transfer it to a mixing bowl. Reserve the coconut water for other uses or discard.
3. In a small bowl, mix together the cornstarch and a couple of tablespoons of the chilled coconut milk until smooth.
4. In a saucepan, combine the remaining coconut milk, brown sugar (or coconut sugar), vanilla extract, and a pinch of salt. Heat the mixture over medium heat until it begins to simmer, stirring occasionally.
5. Once simmering, add the cornstarch mixture to the saucepan, stirring constantly until the mixture thickens slightly, about 2-3 minutes.
6. Remove the saucepan from the heat and let the mixture cool to room temperature.
7. Once cooled, transfer the mixture to an ice cream maker and churn according to the manufacturer's instructions.
8. During the last few minutes of churning, add in the chopped pecans.
9. If you prefer a firmer texture, transfer the churned ice cream to a freezer-safe container, cover it with a lid or plastic wrap, and freeze for at least 4-6 hours, or until firm.
10. Before serving, let the ice cream sit at room temperature for a few minutes to soften slightly. Then scoop it into bowls or cones, and enjoy your Vegan Butter Pecan Ice Cream!

This recipe yields a creamy and indulgent vegan ice cream with the rich flavor of butter pecan, making it a delightful treat for anyone, regardless of dietary preferences!

Lemon Poppy Seed Dairy-Free Ice Cream

Ingredients:

- 2 cans (13.5 oz each) full-fat coconut milk, chilled overnight in the refrigerator
- Zest of 2 lemons
- 1/2 cup freshly squeezed lemon juice (about 4-5 lemons)
- 1/2 cup maple syrup or agave nectar
- 1 teaspoon vanilla extract
- 2 tablespoons poppy seeds

Instructions:

1. Before you begin, make sure to place the cans of coconut milk in the refrigerator overnight to chill.
2. Once chilled, open the cans of coconut milk without shaking them. Scoop out the solid coconut cream that has risen to the top and transfer it to a mixing bowl. Reserve the coconut water for other uses or discard.
3. Add the lemon zest, freshly squeezed lemon juice, maple syrup or agave nectar, and vanilla extract to the coconut cream. Use a hand mixer or stand mixer to beat the mixture on medium-high speed until it becomes smooth and creamy, about 2-3 minutes.
4. Taste the mixture and adjust the sweetness or lemon flavor to your liking, if necessary.
5. Gently fold in the poppy seeds until evenly distributed throughout the mixture.
6. Transfer the mixture to an ice cream maker and churn according to the manufacturer's instructions until it reaches a soft-serve consistency.
7. If you prefer a firmer texture, transfer the churned ice cream to a freezer-safe container, cover it with a lid or plastic wrap, and freeze for at least 4-6 hours, or until firm.
8. Before serving, let the ice cream sit at room temperature for a few minutes to soften slightly. Then scoop it into bowls or cones, and enjoy your Lemon Poppy Seed Dairy-Free Ice Cream!

This recipe creates a creamy and refreshing dairy-free ice cream with the bright and zesty flavors of lemon combined with the subtle crunch of poppy seeds. It's a perfect treat for hot summer days or anytime you're craving a citrusy dessert!

Chocolate Covered Strawberry Dairy-Free Ice Cream

Ingredients:

- 2 cans (13.5 oz each) full-fat coconut milk, chilled overnight in the refrigerator
- 2 cups fresh strawberries, hulled and chopped
- 1/2 cup dairy-free chocolate chips or chopped dark chocolate
- 1/3 cup maple syrup or agave nectar
- 1 teaspoon vanilla extract
- Pinch of salt

Instructions:

1. Before you begin, make sure to place the cans of coconut milk in the refrigerator overnight to chill.
2. Once chilled, open the cans of coconut milk without shaking them. Scoop out the solid coconut cream that has risen to the top and transfer it to a mixing bowl. Reserve the coconut water for other uses or discard.
3. In a blender or food processor, puree the chopped strawberries until smooth.
4. In a small saucepan, melt the dairy-free chocolate chips or chopped dark chocolate over low heat, stirring constantly until smooth. Set aside to cool slightly.
5. Add the strawberry puree, maple syrup or agave nectar, vanilla extract, and a pinch of salt to the coconut cream. Use a hand mixer or stand mixer to beat the mixture on medium-high speed until it becomes smooth and creamy, about 2-3 minutes.
6. Fold in the melted chocolate until evenly distributed throughout the mixture.
7. Transfer the mixture to an ice cream maker and churn according to the manufacturer's instructions until it reaches a soft-serve consistency.
8. If you prefer a firmer texture, transfer the churned ice cream to a freezer-safe container, cover it with a lid or plastic wrap, and freeze for at least 4-6 hours, or until firm.

9. Before serving, let the ice cream sit at room temperature for a few minutes to soften slightly. Then scoop it into bowls or cones, and enjoy your Chocolate Covered Strawberry Dairy-Free Ice Cream!

This recipe combines the classic flavors of chocolate-covered strawberries with creamy dairy-free coconut milk for a decadent and indulgent frozen treat that's perfect for any occasion!

Coconut Pineapple Sorbet

Ingredients:

- 1 cup coconut milk
- 2 cups fresh or canned pineapple chunks
- 1/2 cup sugar (adjust according to taste)
- 1 tablespoon lime juice
- Optional: shredded coconut for garnish

Instructions:

1. Prepare the Pineapple: If using fresh pineapple, peel and core it, then cut it into chunks. If using canned pineapple, drain the chunks.
2. Blend Ingredients: In a blender or food processor, combine the coconut milk, pineapple chunks, sugar, and lime juice. Blend until smooth.
3. Taste and Adjust: Taste the mixture and adjust the sweetness by adding more sugar if desired. Blend again to combine.
4. Chill: Pour the mixture into a shallow dish or ice cream maker. Cover and chill in the refrigerator for at least 2 hours, or until completely cold.
5. Freeze: If you have an ice cream maker, churn the mixture according to the manufacturer's instructions until it reaches a sorbet-like consistency. If you don't have an ice cream maker, you can pour the mixture into a shallow dish and freeze it, stirring every 30 minutes until it's frozen and has a sorbet-like texture.
6. Serve: Once the sorbet is ready, scoop it into bowls or glasses. You can garnish with shredded coconut for an extra tropical touch if desired.

Enjoy your refreshing coconut pineapple sorbet!

Blueberry Cheesecake Dairy-Free Ice Cream

Ingredients:

For the blueberry swirl:

- 2 cups fresh or frozen blueberries
- 1/4 cup granulated sugar
- 1 tablespoon lemon juice
- 1 tablespoon water

For the ice cream base:

- 1 (14 oz) can full-fat coconut milk
- 1 (14 oz) can coconut cream
- 1/2 cup granulated sugar
- 1 teaspoon vanilla extract
- 1/2 cup vegan cream cheese, softened
- 1/2 cup crushed vegan graham crackers or cookies (optional)

Instructions:

1. Prepare the Blueberry Swirl: In a saucepan, combine the blueberries, sugar, lemon juice, and water. Cook over medium heat, stirring occasionally, until the blueberries break down and the mixture thickens, about 10-15 minutes. Remove from heat and let it cool.
2. Make the Ice Cream Base: In a mixing bowl, whisk together the coconut milk, coconut cream, sugar, and vanilla extract until well combined. If you prefer a smoother texture, you can blend these ingredients in a blender until smooth.
3. Add Cream Cheese: Add the softened vegan cream cheese to the coconut milk mixture and whisk until smooth and creamy.
4. Chill: Cover the mixture and chill it in the refrigerator for at least 2 hours, or until completely cold.
5. Churn: Pour the chilled mixture into an ice cream maker and churn according to the manufacturer's instructions until it reaches a soft-serve consistency.

6. Assemble: Once the ice cream has churned, layer it into a container, alternating with spoonfuls of the blueberry swirl and crushed vegan graham crackers or cookies if using. Swirl gently with a spoon or spatula to create a marbled effect.
7. Freeze: Cover the container with a lid or plastic wrap and freeze the ice cream for at least 4-6 hours, or until firm.
8. Serve: Scoop the blueberry cheesecake dairy-free ice cream into bowls or cones and enjoy!

This creamy and indulgent dessert is perfect for satisfying your sweet tooth while being dairy-free!

Raspberry Lemonade Dairy-Free Ice Cream

Ingredients:

For the raspberry swirl:

- 2 cups fresh or frozen raspberries
- 1/4 cup granulated sugar
- 1 tablespoon lemon juice
- 1 tablespoon water

For the ice cream base:

- 1 (14 oz) can full-fat coconut milk
- 1 (14 oz) can coconut cream
- 1/2 cup granulated sugar
- Zest of 1 lemon
- 1/4 cup lemon juice (about 2-3 lemons)
- 1 teaspoon vanilla extract

Instructions:

1. Prepare the Raspberry Swirl: In a saucepan, combine the raspberries, sugar, lemon juice, and water. Cook over medium heat, stirring occasionally, until the raspberries break down and the mixture thickens, about 10-15 minutes. Remove from heat and let it cool.
2. Make the Ice Cream Base: In a mixing bowl, whisk together the coconut milk, coconut cream, sugar, lemon zest, lemon juice, and vanilla extract until well combined.
3. Chill: Cover the mixture and chill it in the refrigerator for at least 2 hours, or until completely cold.
4. Churn: Pour the chilled mixture into an ice cream maker and churn according to the manufacturer's instructions until it reaches a soft-serve consistency.

5. Assemble: Once the ice cream has churned, layer it into a container, alternating with spoonfuls of the raspberry swirl. Swirl gently with a spoon or spatula to create a marbled effect.
6. Freeze: Cover the container with a lid or plastic wrap and freeze the ice cream for at least 4-6 hours, or until firm.
7. Serve: Scoop the raspberry lemonade dairy-free ice cream into bowls or cones and enjoy!

This delightful combination of tangy lemon and sweet raspberry will surely cool you down on a hot day.

Coconut Rum Raisin Dairy-Free Ice Cream

Ingredients:

- 1 (14 oz) can full-fat coconut milk
- 1 (14 oz) can coconut cream
- 1/2 cup granulated sugar
- 1 teaspoon vanilla extract
- 1/4 cup dark rum (adjust to taste)
- 1/2 cup raisins

Instructions:

1. Prepare the Raisins: Place the raisins in a small bowl and cover them with warm water. Let them soak for about 10-15 minutes to plump up. After soaking, drain the raisins and pat them dry with a paper towel.
2. Make the Ice Cream Base: In a mixing bowl, whisk together the coconut milk, coconut cream, sugar, and vanilla extract until well combined.
3. Add Rum: Stir in the dark rum until fully incorporated into the mixture.
4. Chill: Cover the mixture and chill it in the refrigerator for at least 2 hours, or until completely cold.
5. Churn: Pour the chilled mixture into an ice cream maker and churn according to the manufacturer's instructions until it reaches a soft-serve consistency.
6. Add Raisins: In the last few minutes of churning, add the soaked and dried raisins to the ice cream maker. Let them mix in evenly.
7. Freeze: Transfer the churned ice cream into a freezer-safe container. Cover with a lid or plastic wrap and freeze for at least 4-6 hours, or until firm.
8. Serve: Scoop the coconut rum raisin dairy-free ice cream into bowls or cones and enjoy!

This creamy and flavorful ice cream is perfect for those who love the tropical taste of coconut and a hint of rum, with the added sweetness of plump raisins.

Chocolate Mint Dairy-Free Ice Cream

Ingredients:

- 2 (14 oz) cans full-fat coconut milk
- 1/2 cup cocoa powder (unsweetened)
- 1/2 cup granulated sugar (adjust to taste)
- 1 teaspoon vanilla extract
- 1 teaspoon peppermint extract
- 1/2 cup dairy-free chocolate chips or chopped dark chocolate

Instructions:

1. Mix Ingredients: In a saucepan over medium heat, whisk together the coconut milk, cocoa powder, and sugar until well combined and the mixture is smooth.
2. Heat: Cook the mixture, stirring constantly, until it starts to simmer. Remove from heat.
3. Add Flavorings: Stir in the vanilla extract and peppermint extract until fully incorporated. Taste and adjust the sweetness or mint flavor as desired.
4. Cool: Allow the mixture to cool to room temperature. Then, transfer it to a bowl or container and refrigerate until completely chilled, about 2-3 hours or overnight.
5. Churn: Once chilled, pour the mixture into an ice cream maker and churn according to the manufacturer's instructions until it reaches a soft-serve consistency.
6. Add Chocolate: In the last few minutes of churning, add the dairy-free chocolate chips or chopped dark chocolate to the ice cream maker. Let them mix in evenly.
7. Freeze: Transfer the churned ice cream into a freezer-safe container. Cover with a lid or plastic wrap and freeze for at least 4-6 hours, or until firm.
8. Serve: Scoop the chocolate mint dairy-free ice cream into bowls or cones and enjoy!

This creamy and refreshing dessert combines the richness of chocolate with the coolness of mint, creating a delightful treat that's perfect for any occasion.

Strawberry Kiwi Sorbet

Ingredients:

- 2 cups fresh strawberries, hulled and sliced
- 2 kiwi fruits, peeled and sliced
- 1/2 cup granulated sugar
- 1/4 cup water
- 1 tablespoon lemon juice

Instructions:

1. Prepare Fruit: Place the sliced strawberries and kiwi fruits in a blender or food processor.
2. Make Simple Syrup: In a small saucepan, combine the sugar and water. Heat over medium heat, stirring occasionally, until the sugar is completely dissolved. Remove from heat and let it cool slightly.
3. Blend: Pour the simple syrup over the strawberries and kiwi in the blender. Add the lemon juice. Blend until smooth.
4. Strain (Optional): If you prefer a smoother sorbet, you can strain the mixture through a fine-mesh sieve to remove any seeds or pulp. This step is optional.
5. Chill: Transfer the mixture to a shallow dish and refrigerate for at least 2 hours, or until completely chilled.
6. Churn: Once chilled, pour the mixture into an ice cream maker and churn according to the manufacturer's instructions until it reaches a sorbet-like consistency.
7. Freeze: Transfer the churned sorbet into a freezer-safe container. Cover with a lid or plastic wrap and freeze for at least 4 hours, or until firm.
8. Serve: Scoop the strawberry kiwi sorbet into bowls or cones and enjoy the refreshing combination of flavors!

This sorbet is not only delicious but also a vibrant and colorful dessert that's perfect for hot summer days or anytime you're craving something fruity and sweet.

Key Lime Pie Dairy-Free Ice Cream

Ingredients:

- 1 (14 oz) can full-fat coconut milk
- 1 (14 oz) can coconut cream
- 1/2 cup granulated sugar
- Zest of 3 limes
- 1/2 cup fresh key lime juice (about 10-12 key limes)
- 1 teaspoon vanilla extract
- 1/2 cup crushed graham crackers (use gluten-free if needed)

Instructions:

1. Prepare Lime Zest and Juice: Zest the limes and then juice them to get 1/2 cup of fresh key lime juice. Set aside.
2. Make the Ice Cream Base: In a mixing bowl, whisk together the coconut milk, coconut cream, sugar, lime zest, lime juice, and vanilla extract until well combined.
3. Chill: Cover the mixture and chill it in the refrigerator for at least 2 hours, or until completely cold.
4. Churn: Pour the chilled mixture into an ice cream maker and churn according to the manufacturer's instructions until it reaches a soft-serve consistency.
5. Add Graham Crackers: In the last few minutes of churning, add the crushed graham crackers to the ice cream maker. Let them mix in evenly.
6. Freeze: Transfer the churned ice cream into a freezer-safe container. Cover with a lid or plastic wrap and freeze for at least 4-6 hours, or until firm.
7. Serve: Scoop the key lime pie dairy-free ice cream into bowls or cones and enjoy!

This creamy and tangy dessert captures the flavors of a classic key lime pie, with the added crunch of graham crackers. It's perfect for cooling down on a hot day or enjoying as a refreshing treat anytime!

Mango Pineapple Coconut Milk Ice Cream

Ingredients:

- 2 ripe mangoes, peeled, pitted, and diced
- 1 cup pineapple chunks (fresh or canned, drained)
- 1 (14 oz) can full-fat coconut milk
- 1/4 cup granulated sugar (adjust to taste)
- 1 teaspoon vanilla extract
- Optional: shredded coconut for garnish

Instructions:

1. Prepare the Fruits: Peel and dice the mangoes, and prepare the pineapple chunks. If using canned pineapple, make sure to drain the chunks before using.
2. Blend: In a blender or food processor, combine the diced mangoes, pineapple chunks, coconut milk, sugar, and vanilla extract. Blend until smooth and well combined.
3. Taste and Adjust: Taste the mixture and adjust the sweetness by adding more sugar if desired. Blend again to incorporate.
4. Chill: Pour the mixture into a shallow dish and cover it. Place it in the refrigerator to chill for at least 2 hours, or until completely cold.
5. Churn: Once chilled, pour the mixture into an ice cream maker and churn according to the manufacturer's instructions until it reaches a soft-serve consistency.
6. Freeze: Transfer the churned ice cream into a freezer-safe container. Optionally, sprinkle some shredded coconut on top for added texture and flavor. Cover with a lid or plastic wrap and freeze for at least 4-6 hours, or until firm.
7. Serve: Scoop the mango pineapple coconut milk ice cream into bowls or cones, and enjoy the tropical flavors!

This creamy and fruity dairy-free ice cream is perfect for enjoying the taste of summer all year round.

Vegan Snickers Ice Cream

Ingredients:

For the ice cream base:

- 2 (14 oz) cans full-fat coconut milk
- 1/2 cup granulated sugar (adjust to taste)
- 1 teaspoon vanilla extract

For the caramel sauce:

- 1 cup pitted dates, soaked in warm water for 15 minutes
- 1/4 cup almond butter
- 1/4 cup coconut cream
- Pinch of salt

For the mix-ins:

- 1/2 cup roasted peanuts, roughly chopped
- 1/2 cup vegan chocolate chips or chopped dark chocolate

Instructions:

1. Prepare the Ice Cream Base:
    - In a mixing bowl, whisk together the coconut milk, sugar, and vanilla extract until well combined.
    - Pour the mixture into an ice cream maker and churn according to the manufacturer's instructions until it reaches a soft-serve consistency.
2. Make the Caramel Sauce:
    - In a food processor or blender, combine the soaked dates (drained), almond butter, coconut cream, and salt. Blend until smooth and creamy. If the mixture is too thick, you can add a tablespoon or two of water to thin it out.

- Transfer the caramel sauce to a bowl and set aside.
3. Assemble the Ice Cream:
    - Once the ice cream reaches a soft-serve consistency, transfer half of it to a freezer-safe container.
    - Drizzle half of the caramel sauce over the ice cream, then sprinkle half of the chopped peanuts and chocolate chips on top.
    - Repeat with the remaining ice cream, caramel sauce, peanuts, and chocolate chips.
    - Use a spoon or spatula to gently swirl the caramel sauce and mix-ins into the ice cream.
4. Freeze:
    - Cover the container with a lid or plastic wrap and freeze for at least 4-6 hours, or until firm.
5. Serve:
    - Scoop the vegan Snickers ice cream into bowls or cones and enjoy the creamy, caramel, and nutty goodness!

This vegan Snickers ice cream is a decadent treat that's perfect for satisfying your sweet cravings while keeping it plant-based.

Lemon Basil Dairy-Free Ice Cream

Ingredients:

- 2 (14 oz) cans full-fat coconut milk
- 1/2 cup granulated sugar (adjust to taste)
- Zest of 2 lemons
- 1/2 cup fresh lemon juice (about 4-6 lemons)
- 1/4 cup fresh basil leaves, chopped
- 1 teaspoon vanilla extract

Instructions:

1. Prepare Ingredients:
    - Zest the lemons and squeeze out the juice. Chop the fresh basil leaves.
2. Make the Ice Cream Base:
    - In a mixing bowl, whisk together the coconut milk, sugar, lemon zest, lemon juice, chopped basil leaves, and vanilla extract until well combined.
3. Chill:
    - Cover the mixture and chill it in the refrigerator for at least 2 hours, or until completely cold.
4. Churn:
    - Once chilled, pour the mixture into an ice cream maker and churn according to the manufacturer's instructions until it reaches a soft-serve consistency.
5. Freeze:
    - Transfer the churned ice cream into a freezer-safe container.
    - Cover with a lid or plastic wrap and freeze for at least 4-6 hours, or until firm.
6. Serve:
    - Scoop the lemon basil dairy-free ice cream into bowls or cones and enjoy the refreshing combination of lemon and basil flavors!

This dairy-free ice cream is light, creamy, and bursting with the citrusy zing of lemon and the aromatic freshness of basil. It's a perfect dessert for hot summer days or anytime you're craving a unique and flavorful treat.

Hazelnut Chocolate Swirl Dairy-Free Ice Cream

Ingredients:

For the ice cream base:

- 2 (14 oz) cans full-fat coconut milk
- 1/2 cup granulated sugar (adjust to taste)
- 1 teaspoon vanilla extract
- 1/2 cup hazelnut butter or hazelnut spread (make sure it's dairy-free)

For the chocolate swirl:

- 1/2 cup dairy-free chocolate chips or chopped dark chocolate
- 2 tablespoons coconut oil

Instructions:

1. Make the Ice Cream Base:
    - In a mixing bowl, whisk together the coconut milk, sugar, and vanilla extract until well combined.
    - Stir in the hazelnut butter or hazelnut spread until fully incorporated into the mixture.
2. Chill:
    - Cover the mixture and chill it in the refrigerator for at least 2 hours, or until completely cold.
3. Churn:
    - Once chilled, pour the mixture into an ice cream maker and churn according to the manufacturer's instructions until it reaches a soft-serve consistency.
4. Make the Chocolate Swirl:
    - In a small saucepan, melt the dairy-free chocolate chips or chopped dark chocolate with the coconut oil over low heat, stirring constantly until smooth. Remove from heat and let it cool slightly.
5. Assemble:

- Once the ice cream reaches a soft-serve consistency, transfer half of it to a freezer-safe container.
- Drizzle half of the chocolate swirl mixture over the ice cream.
- Repeat with the remaining ice cream and chocolate swirl, layering them in the container.
- Use a knife or spatula to gently swirl the chocolate mixture into the ice cream, creating a marbled effect.

6. Freeze:
    - Cover the container with a lid or plastic wrap and freeze for at least 4-6 hours, or until firm.
7. Serve:
    - Scoop the hazelnut chocolate swirl dairy-free ice cream into bowls or cones and enjoy the rich and creamy flavors!

This dairy-free ice cream is sure to satisfy your cravings for something sweet and indulgent, with the irresistible combination of hazelnut and chocolate swirls.

www.ingramcontent.com/pod-product-compliance
Lightning Source LLC
LaVergne TN
LVHW081608060526
838201LV00054B/2142